COLLECTION

Big Data

BIG DATA
700 questions

Volume 2

Prof. Marcão - Marcus Vinícius Pinto

Disclaimer:

ISBN: 9798311061322

Publishing imprint: Independently published

Summary.

1   FOREWORD.   **9**

1.1   WHY CHOOSE 'BIG DATA: 700 QUESTIONS'?   9
1.2   WHO IS THIS COLLECTION FOR?   9
1.3   WHAT MAKES THIS COLLECTION UNIQUE?   9
1.4   THE FUTURE BELONGS TO THOSE WHO MASTER THE DATA.   10
1.5   BE PART OF THE DATA REVOLUTION!   10
1.6   THE 700 QUESTIONS COLLECTION.   11
1.6.1   BIG DATA: 700 QUESTIONS - VOLUME 1.   11
1.6.2   BIG DATA: 700 QUESTIONS - VOLUME 2.   11
1.6.3   BIG DATA: 700 QUESTIONS - VOLUME 3.   11
1.6.4   BIG DATA: 700 QUESTIONS - VOLUME 4.   12
1.6.5   BIG DATA: 700 QUESTIONS - VOLUME 5.   12

2   INFORMATION SCIENCE.   **13**

2.1   QUESTIONS.   **13**
2.2   TEMPLATE.   **31**

3   DATA AND ANALYTICS TECHNOLOGY TRENDS.   **35**

3.1   QUESTIONS.   **35**
3.2   ANSWERS.   **49**

4   AUGMENTED ANALYTICS.   **52**

4.1   QUESTIONS.   **52**
4.2   ANSWERS.   **56**

5   CONTINUOUS INTELLIGENCE.   **57**

5.1	**QUESTIONS.**	**57**
5.2	**ANSWERS.**	**65**

6	**DISTRIBUTED COMPUTING.**	**67**

6.1	**QUESTIONS.**	**67**
6.2	**ANSWERS.**	**72**

7	**LATENCY.**	**74**

7.1	**QUESTIONS.**	**74**
7.2	**ANSWERS.**	**76**

8	**CONCLUSION.**	**77**

9	**BIBLIOGRAPHY.**	**79**

10	**BIG DATA COLLECTION: UNLOCKING THE FUTURE OF DATA IN AN ESSENTIAL COLLECTION.**	**85**

10.1	**WHO IS THE BIG DATA COLLECTION FOR.**	**86**
10.2	**GET TO KNOW THE BOOKS IN THE COLLECTION.**	**87**
10.2.1	SIMPLIFYING BIG DATA INTO 7 CHAPTERS.	87
10.2.2	BIG DATA MANAGEMENT.	88
10.2.3	BIG DATA ARCHITECTURE.	88
10.2.4	BIG DATA IMPLEMENTATION.	88
10.2.5	STRATEGIES TO REDUCE COSTS AND MAXIMIZE BIG DATA INVESTMENTS.	89
10.2.6	700 BIG DATA QUESTIONS COLLECTION.	89
10.2.7	BIG DATA GLOSSARY.	90

11 DISCOVER THE "ARTIFICIAL INTELLIGENCE AND THE POWER OF DATA" COLLECTION – AN INVITATION TO TRANSFORM YOUR CAREER AND KNOWLEDGE. 92

11.1 WHY BUY THIS COLLECTION? 92
11.2 TARGET AUDIENCE OF THIS COLLECTION? 93
11.3 MUCH MORE THAN TECHNIQUE – A COMPLETE TRANSFORMATION. 93

12 THE BOOKS OF THE COLLECTION. 94

12.1 DATA, INFORMATION AND KNOWLEDGE IN THE ERA OF ARTIFICIAL INTELLIGENCE. 94
12.2 FROM DATA TO GOLD: HOW TO TURN INFORMATION INTO WISDOM IN THE AGE OF AI. 94
12.3 CHALLENGES AND LIMITATIONS OF DATA IN AI. 94
12.4 HISTORICAL DATA IN DATABASES FOR AI: STRUCTURES, PRESERVATION, AND PURGE. 95
12.5 CONTROLLED VOCABULARY FOR DATA DICTIONARY: A COMPLETE GUIDE. 95
12.6 DATA CURATION AND MANAGEMENT FOR THE AGE OF AI. 95
12.7 INFORMATION ARCHITECTURE. 95
12.8 FUNDAMENTALS: THE ESSENTIALS OF MASTERING ARTIFICIAL INTELLIGENCE. 95
12.9 LLMS - LARGE-SCALE LANGUAGE MODELS. 96
12.10 MACHINE LEARNING: FUNDAMENTALS AND ADVANCES. 96
12.11 INSIDE SYNTHETIC MINDS. 96
12.12 THE ISSUE OF COPYRIGHT. 96
12.13 1121 QUESTIONS AND ANSWERS: FROM BASIC TO COMPLEX – PART 1 TO 4. 96
12.14 THE DEFINITIVE GLOSSARY OF ARTIFICIAL INTELLIGENCE. 97
12.15 PROMPT ENGINEERING - VOLUMES 1 TO 6. 97
12.16 GUIDE TO BEING A PROMPT ENGINEER – VOLUMES 1 AND 2. 98
12.17 DATA GOVERNANCE WITH AI – VOLUMES 1 TO 3. 98
12.18 ALGORITHM GOVERNANCE. 98
12.19 FROM IT PROFESSIONAL TO AI EXPERT: THE ULTIMATE GUIDE TO A SUCCESSFUL CAREER TRANSITION. 99
12.20 INTELLIGENT LEADERSHIP WITH AI: TRANSFORM YOUR TEAM AND DRIVE RESULTS. 99
12.21 IMPACTS AND TRANSFORMATIONS: COMPLETE COLLECTION. 99

12.22   BIG DATA WITH AI: COMPLETE COLLECTION.   **100**

13   ABOUT THE AUTHOR.   **101**

14   HOW TO CONTACT PROF. MARCÃO.   **103**

14.1   FOR LECTURES, TRAINING AND BUSINESS MENTORING.   **103**
14.2   PROF. MARCÃO, ON LINKEDIN.   **103**

1   Foreword.

Imagine yourself mastering the secrets of Big Data, the driving force behind the most impactful decisions in the modern world. The "BIG DATA: 700 Questions" collection is more than a book series – it is a definitive guide, an intellectual challenge, and an invitation to explore data science in an in-depth and interactive way. Part of the "Big Data" collection, this work offers a structured path for those who want not only to understand, but also to apply knowledge about data in their career, business, or studies.

1.1   Why choose 'BIG DATA: 700 Questions'?

This collection is designed to provide dynamic, challenging, and hands-on learning. With 700 questions strategically crafted and distributed in 5 volumes, it allows you to advance in the domain of Big Data in a progressive and engaging way. Each answer is an opportunity to expand your vision and apply concepts realistically and effectively.

1.2   Who is this collection for?

1   Technology and Data Analysis Professionals: Expand your skills and become a valued expert in the market, where fluency in data is one of the most sought-after differentials.

2   Executives and Decision Makers: Understand how data can drive business strategies, improve operational efficiency, and generate competitive advantage.

3   Students and Researchers: Build a strong foundation for your academic or professional career by preparing for the challenges and opportunities of the digital age.

4   Knowledge Enthusiasts: If you're curious about how data shapes the world, this collection offers complete immersion, ranging from fundamental concepts to advanced topics.

1.3   What makes this collection unique?

✅ Active and Interactive Learning.

Each question challenges your comprehension and encourages critical reflection, transforming reading into a continuous learning experience.

🎯 Practical and Applicable Approach.

The answers go beyond theory, showing real-world applications in a variety of industries, including business, government, education, and research.

🔍 360° view of Big Data.

Delve into not only the techniques and tools, but also the ethical, legal, and social implications of using data.

📊 Data Literacy Development.,

The digital age requires professionals who know how to interpret, question, and transform data into powerful insights. This book will help you develop this essential skill.

1.4   The Future Belongs to Those Who Master the Data.

Big Data is no longer a trend – it is a consolidated and essential reality for all areas of knowledge and the market. Companies, governments, and educational institutions are increasingly dependent on data analysis to make informed decisions. Investing in your learning today means preparing for a future of limitless opportunities.

With 'BIG DATA: 700 Questions', you will always be one step ahead, acquiring not only knowledge, but also the ability to apply it strategically and innovatively.

1.5   Be Part of the Data Revolution!

Don't be left behind. The Big Data revolution has already begun, and this collection is your passport to a universe of possibilities. Purchase the "BIG DATA: 700 Questions" collection now and turn your curiosity into action, your information into understanding and your questions into solutions that shape the future.

The future is for data. Your place in it starts now!

1.6   The 700 questions collection.

The collection consists of the following books:

1.6.1   BIG DATA: 700 Questions - Volume 1.

It deals with information as the raw material for everything, the fundamental concepts and applications of Big Data.

1.6.2   BIG DATA: 700 Questions - Volume 2.

It addresses Big Data in the context of information science, data technology trends and analytics, Augmented analytics, continuous intelligence, distributed computing, and latency.

1.6.3   BIG DATA: 700 Questions - Volume 3.

It contemplates the technological and management aspects of Big Data, data mining, classification trees, logistic regression and professions in the context of Big Data.

1.6.4 BIG DATA: 700 Questions - Volume 4.

It deals with the requirements for Big Data management, the data structures used, the architecture and storage layers, Business Intelligence in the context of Big Data, and application virtualization.

1.6.5 BIG DATA: 700 Questions - Volume 5.

The book deals with SAAS, IAAS AND PAAS, Big Data implementation, overhead and hidden costs, Big Data for small businesses, digital security and data warehousing in the context of Big Data.

Happy studying!

Prof. Marcão - Marcus Vinícius Pinto

M.Sc. in Information Technology
Specialist in Information Technology.
Consultant, Mentor and Speaker on Artificial Intelligence,
Information Architecture and Data Governance.
Founder, CEO, teacher and
pedagogical advisor at MVP Consult.

2 Information Science.

2.1 Questions.

1. What is the main objective of Information Science in the context of Big Data?

   A) Store information without worrying about its future usability.

   B) Ensure that all information is published in printed formats.

   C) Facilitate the understanding, processing and extraction of value from large volumes of data.

   D) Limit access to data to maintain the exclusivity of information.

2. How can Information Science help with privacy issues related to Big Data?

   A) Encouraging the collection of data without users' consent.

   B) Developing policies and technologies to protect sensitive information.

   C) Ignoring data protection laws and regulations.

   D) Storing all data openly and publicly.

3. What does the term "open data" mean in the world of Big Data?

   A) Data that is publicly available without any restriction on access or use.

   B) Data that is physically open and spread across multiple locations.

C) Confidential information that has been compromised.

D) Databases that are technically defective and cannot be closed.

4. What is the relationship between Information Science and cloud computing in the use of Big Data?

A) Information Science rejects cloud computing because it is a very advanced technology.

B) Cloud computing offers resources for data storage and analysis, facilitated by Information Science.

C) They are totally disconnected fields with no mutual influence.

D) Cloud computing is seen as a passing fad with no relevance to Big Data.

5. What role does metadata play in Information Science applied to Big Data?

A) They are seen as an unnecessary nuisance and generally ignored.

B) Provides contextual information that helps in the organization and interpretation of primary data

C) They represent an excess of details that complicates the analysis of the data.

D) They have the sole purpose of increasing the volume of stored data.

6. In the world of Big Data, how is the term 'interoperability' important to Information Science?

   A) Means the ability to keep data isolated across different systems.

   B) It is relevant only for printed data and not for digital data.

   C) It refers to the ability to integrate and use data from different sources and formats efficiently.

   D) It represents an outdated trend that is no longer considered in Information Science.

7. What is the role of data curation in Information Science within the Big Data environment?

   A) Decorate and visually embellish the data sets.

   B) Ensure that data is preserved without the need for analysis.

   C) Select, maintain and ensure access to important data for present and future use.

   D) Keep the data hidden to prevent any analysis or interpretation.

8. How does Information Science contribute to predictive analytics in Big Data?

   A) Emphasizing the study of historical texts to the detriment of predictive models.

   B) Focusing exclusively on short-term forecasts without a basis in data.

C) Integrating different data sources and applying statistical techniques to predict future trends.

D) Limiting itself only to cataloguing and archiving old data.

9. What characterizes the ethical dimension of Information Science in the context of Big Data?

A) The promotion of the use of data without considering the moral implications.

B) The concern with the responsible and ethical use of data, including issues of consent and privacy.

C) The complete release of access to personal data, aiming at total transparency.

D) Ethics is disregarded, focusing only on profit maximization.

10. How is the concept of data literacy relevant in the world of Big Data?

A) It is not relevant, as the data analysis should be left to experts.

B) Data literacy is crucial to empower individuals to understand and use data effectively in their decisions.

C) Refers exclusively to the ability to read and write text in databases.

D) It is a secondary concern, because Big Data software is completely autonomous.

11. What is the importance of data patterns in Information Science for Big Data?

A) They are irrelevant, because each set of data must be unique.

B) Standards complicate data sharing between different systems.

C) Standards facilitate interoperability, sharing, and reuse of data between disparate systems.

D) Standards are only useful for data that will not be shared or analyzed.

12. Which of the following is a challenge in big data management?

A) The need to reduce the amount of data stored.

B) The rapid obsolescence of data storage technology.

C) The trivial configuration of data privacy and security.

D) Managing the integrity, security, and accessibility of data as it grows in volume and complexity.

13. How is digital curation applied in the field of Big Data?

A) Removing all digital content to keep only analog data.

B) Preservation, organizing, and long-term maintaining digital data to ensure its continued access.

C) Displaying digital data in art galleries or museums.

D) Limiting the amount of data made available digitally.

14. In the field of Big Data, what is cognitive informatics?

    A) An antiquated approach to data processing.

    B) Systems that simulate human thinking to analyze and interpret large volumes of data in an intelligent way.

    C) The practice of avoiding any use of digital data in cognitive analysis.

    D) A field of computer science focused on basic cognitive functions such as visual perception and memorization.

15. What are the ethical implications involved in the use of Big Data in Information Science?

    A) There are no ethical implications, as data is neutral in nature.

    B) Ethical implications are addressed only if there are legal problems.

    C) It involves issues such as privacy, informed consent, and the fair use of information.

    D) It is focused exclusively on efficiency gains, without ethical considerations.

16. What is the impact of fake news in the context of Big Data and Information Science?

    A) They are beneficial, as they increase the amount of data available.

B) They have no impact at all, as the algorithms can automatically recognize and ignore.

C) They can distort analyses and decisions when mixed with truthful data.

D) They are readily identified and do not affect the field of Big Data.

17. How does Information Science ensure the sustainability of Big Data?

A) Ignoring sustainability in favor of technological advancement.

B) Encouraging the incessant addition of new data without considering obsolescence.

C) Through practices such as data curation and efficient management of computational resources.

D) Ensuring that all storage devices are produced with non-recyclable materials.

18. What is the relationship between Information Science and Artificial Intelligence in the context of Big Data?

A) Information Science precedes and excludes any application of Artificial Intelligence.

B) Artificial Intelligence is a completely separate area with no connections to Information Science.

C) Artificial Intelligence is a crucial tool within Information Science to analyze and interpret large volumes of data.

D) Uses Artificial Intelligence methods only for data security purposes and not for analysis or processing.

19. How does Information Science impact Big Data analytics?

A) Simplifying datasets so that they contain less information.

B) Providing theories and methods for structuring and interpreting complex data.

C) Prioritizing historical data as opposed to new data sets.

D) Focusing only on print publications and ignoring digital data.

20. What is the role of ontology in the world of Big Data according to Information Science?

A) To create classification systems based on biology.

B) Establish a common set of concepts and relationships to better understand the data.

C) Contribute to the development of autonomously aware artificial intelligence.

D) Reduce the volume of data, eliminating those that are considered less important.

21. What does Information Science consider as high-quality data in Big Data?

A) Data that is easily accessible but may not be accurate.

B) Information that is only large in volume, regardless of its accuracy or relevance.

C) Accurate, current, complete and relevant data for the question under study.

D) Any data collected without concern for its subsequent use.

22. How does Information Science promote the ethical use of Big Data?

A) Encouraging the unrestricted use of all types of data, regardless of the source.

B) Advocating governance policies that respect the privacy and consent of individuals.

C) Teaching techniques to hide the origin of data and how to use it indiscriminately.

D) Completely discouraging the use of digital data.

23. What is the importance of indexing in the context of Big Data?

A) Indexing is unnecessary, because Big Data data is naturally organized.

B) It is essential to enable the rapid and effective retrieval of information in large data sets.

C) Its only importance is for the organization of physical libraries and has no place in Big Data.

D) It has an aesthetic function to improve the presentation of data, without impacting information retrieval.

24. How does sentiment analysis relate to Information Science in Big Data?

A) It has no relationship, because it focuses only on the emotional part and not on the factual.

B) It is part of the data mining techniques that determine public perception on certain topics.

C) It is limited to determining the general sentiment of historical documents.

D) It applies only in the context of personal social networks and not in collective data.

25. How has the concept of Big Data changed the focus of Information Science?

A) It led Information Science to focus exclusively on the volume of data.

B) It did not cause changes; Information Science continues with the same focus as before.

C) Expands the scope of Information Science to include large-scale data analysis and management.

D) Reduced the size of data considered significant for research to only smaller, more manageable sets.

26. In Information Science, how has Big Data transformed academic research?

A) Preserved traditional methods and rejected new data technologies.

B) It allowed access to a wider range of data, potentially enriching the research.

C) It focused the research only on technological aspects, ignoring social implications.

D) The value of academic research has decreased, as now everyone has access to the same data.

27. What ethical challenges does Big Data introduce for Information Science?

A) None, as all data collected is anonymous by default.

B) The question of how to ensure data privacy and obtain informed consent from users.

C) Ethical challenges are considered irrelevant, since technological advancement is prioritized.

D) Strictly limit the scope of research to avoid any possibility of ethical dilemma.

28. How do advances in data visualization affect the practice of Information Science in Big Data?

A) They make the interpretation of data more complex and less accessible.

B) They have no impact, because Information Science only deals with data storage.

C) Improve the communication of complex findings, making them more understandable to a wider audience.

D) Reduce the need for analytical skills, as graphs oversimplify data.

29. To what extent does Information Science contribute to data security in Big Data?

A) Focusing primarily on secure physical storage methodologies.

B) Developing and applying protocols and practices to protect data from unauthorized access.

C) Treating data security as an exclusive responsibility of IT departments.

D) Ignoring security principles in favor of free data sharing.

30. What does 'data longevity' represent in the context of Information Science and Big Data?

A) The belief that all data loses relevance quickly.

B) The admission that the data collected will be useful indefinitely, without the need for updating.

C) The effort to ensure that data remains accessible and usable over time, despite technological changes.

D) The data life cycle is irrelevant in Information Science.

31. How does the concept of Big Data redefine the role of librarians and information workers?

A) Making its functions obsolete, as everything is now digitized and automated.

B) Requiring them to acquire new skills in data management, analytics, and information technology to handle large data sets.

C) Promoting a regression to traditional cataloguing and archiving practices.

D) Keeping their functions exactly the same, without any need for adaptation or learning.

32. What kind of impact does Big Data have on academic training in Information Science?

A) It forced the elimination of disciplines related to information technology from the curricula.

B) It had no impact; resumes remain the same as they were before the emergence of Big Data.

C) Introduced the need to teach skills in data analysis, programming and statistics.

D) Reduced the emphasis on digital skills, focusing more on interpersonal skills.

33. How are Information Science and Big Data related to the concept of open data?

    A) Information Science is opposed to the idea of open data for security reasons.

    B) Big Data has made the concept of open data obsolete.

    C) Information Science uses Big Data to promote open data practices, encouraging transparency and public access to data.

    D) Open data is seen as a threat to the concept of Big Data and, therefore, avoided by information professionals.

34. What techniques are employed by Information Science to address the heterogeneity of data in Big Data?

    A) Avoid any kind of standardization to maintain the uniqueness of the data sets.

    B) The application of normalization schemes, data integration and metadata to create consistency.

    C) Promote the use of a single data format, abolishing all others.

    D) Ignore heterogeneity and collect only data that is already in compatible formats.

35. How does Information Science deal with the volume of data generated by Big Data?

    A) Focusing on traditional physical archiving methodologies and ignoring digital data.

B) Developing mass storage strategies that are scalable and cost-effective.

C) Collecting only a representative sample of the data, discarding the excess.

D) Exclusion of old data to make room for new ones, in a process of constant rotation.

36. What are the '3 Vs' of Big Data in Information Science?

A) Vigor, Viability and Advantage – the main objectives when using Big Data.

B) Variety, Velocity and Volume – the characteristics that define the challenges and opportunities of Big Data.

C) Visualization, Verification and Valuation – techniques used to present Big Data data.

D) Virtualization, Variability and Veto – the security principles applied to Big Data.

37. What is the contribution of data mining in the context of Information Science?

A) It is irrelevant, since it does not deal with significant volumes of data.

B) Focuses solely on recovering lost or corrupted data.

C) Offers methods and techniques to discover patterns, trends, and knowledge in large volumes of data.

D) Data mining is used only for financial purposes, without any link to Information Science.

38. What is the challenge of data provenance in Big Data for Information Science professionals?

A) Determining the original source of the data is of lesser importance in Big Data.

B) The provenance of data is irrelevant to Information Science, as all data is treated equally.

C) Trace the origin and history of the data to ensure its authenticity and reliability.

D) Maintain the anonymity of sources, regardless of the need to validate the information.

39. How does Information Science address the issue of scalability in Big Data systems?

A) Scalability is the sole responsibility of the systems engineering team.

B) Working to create frameworks that can expand as the volume of data grows.

C) Limiting the volume of data collected to avoid scalability issues.

D) Ignoring scalability, focusing only on the theoretical aspects of the data.

40. What is the relationship between Big Data and knowledge management in Information Science?

A) Big Data does not affect knowledge management, as they are completely different areas.

B) Big Data provides new opportunities to capture, store and disseminate knowledge effectively.

C) Knowledge management has become less important with the arrival of Big Data.

D) The focus on Big Data has led to the forgetfulness of traditional knowledge management practices.

41. How is predictive analytics in Big Data influenced by Information Science?

A) Predictive analytics is discarded in favor of simpler descriptive analytics.

B) Information Science provides the theoretical foundation for data modeling used in forecasting.

C) As it is an exclusive marketing tool, Information Science does not contribute to predictive analysis.

D) It does not offer contribution, since it is only dedicated to ordering the data and not to interpreting them.

42. In what aspects is data quality a primary focus in Information Science in relation to Big Data?

A) The concern is only in the quantity of data, not in the quality.

B) Professionals are dedicated to improving data quality, focusing on accuracy, completeness, and timeliness.

C) Data quality is relevant only to specific fields, such as health and finance.

D) Quality is set aside to focus on complex statistical analyses.

2.2   Template.

1. C) Facilitate the understanding, processing and extraction of value from large volumes of data.

2. B) Developing policies and technologies to protect sensitive information.

3. A) Data that is publicly available without any restriction on access or use.

4. B) Cloud computing offers resources for data storage and analysis, facilitated by Information Science.

5. B) Provides contextual information that helps in the organization and interpretation of primary data

6. C) It refers to the ability to integrate and use data from different sources and formats efficiently.

7. C) Select, maintain and ensure access to important data for present and future use.

8. C) Integrating different data sources and applying statistical techniques to predict future trends.

9. B) The concern with the responsible and ethical use of data, including issues of consent and privacy.

10. B) Data literacy is crucial to empower individuals to understand and use data effectively in their decisions.

11. C) Standards facilitate interoperability, sharing, and reuse of data

between disparate systems.

12. D) Managing the integrity, security, and accessibility of data as it grows in volume and complexity.

13. B) Preservation, organizing, and long-term maintaining digital data to ensure its continued access.

14. B) Systems that simulate human thought to

15. C) It involves issues such as privacy, informed consent, and the fair use of information.

16. C) They can distort analyses and decisions when mixed with truthful data.

17. C) Through practices such as data curation and efficient management of computational resources.

18. C) Artificial Intelligence is a crucial tool within Information Science to analyze and interpret large volumes of data.

19. B) Providing theories and methods for structuring and interpreting complex data.

20. B) Establish a common set of concepts and relationships to better understand the data.

21. C) Accurate, current, complete and relevant data for the question under study.

22. B) Advocating governance policies that respect the privacy and consent of individuals.

23. B) It is essential to enable the rapid and effective retrieval of information in large data sets.

24. B) It is part of the data mining techniques that determine public perception on certain topics.

25. C) Expands the scope of Information Science to include large-scale data analysis and management.

26. B) It allowed access to a wider range of data, potentially enriching the research.

27. B) The question of how to ensure data privacy and obtain informed consent from users.

28. C) Improve the communication of complex findings, making them more understandable to a wider audience.

29. B) Developing and applying protocols and practices to protect data from unauthorized access.

30. C) The effort to ensure that data remains accessible and usable over time, despite technological changes.

31. B) Requiring them to acquire new skills in data management, analytics, and information technology to handle large data sets.

32. C) Introduced the need to teach skills in data analysis, programming and statistics.

33. C) Information Science uses Big Data to promote open data practices, encouraging transparency and public access to data.

34. B) The application of normalization schemes, data integration and metadata to create consistency.

35. B) Developing mass storage strategies that are scalable and cost-effective.

36. B) Variety, Velocity and Volume – the characteristics that define the challenges and opportunities of Big Data.

37. C) Offers methods and techniques to discover patterns, trends, and knowledge in large volumes of data.

38. C) Trace the origin and history of the data to ensure its authenticity and reliability.

39. B) Working to create frameworks that can expand as the volume of data grows.

40. B) Big Data provides new opportunities to capture, store and disseminate knowledge effectively.

41. B) Information Science provides the theoretical foundation for data modeling used in forecasting.

42. B) Professionals are dedicated to improving data quality, focusing on accuracy, completeness, and timeliness.

3 Data and Analytics Technology Trends.

3.1 Questions.

1. Which data technology trend refers to the massive processing of data of a complex nature, usually in real time?

    A. Data Warehousing.

    B. Data Lakes.

    C. Big Data Analytics.

    D. In-memory Computing.

2. What technology allows you to perform complex analysis and ad-hoc queries on large volumes of data with great speed?

    A. Data Mining.

    B. In-memory Analytics.

    C. ETL (Extract, Transform, Load).

    D. Data Virtualization.

3. What is the Internet of Things (IoT) and how does it relate to data analytics?

    A. A network of physical devices that collect and share electronic data.

    B. A software tool for data visualization.

    C. A method of batch processing large data sets.

D. A data communication protocol.

4. Which trend in analytics refers to artificial intelligence explaining how it came to certain conclusions or results?

A. Prescriptive Analytics.

B. Explainable AI.

C. Cognitive Computing.

D. Automated Machine Learning.

5. What concept describes the data analysis performed directly on the edge devices of the network?

A. Edge Analytics.

B. Cloud Computing.

C. Distributed Data Processing.

D. Quantum Analytics.

6. What trend is driving the need for professionals trained in privacy law and data protection techniques?

A. Data Cleansing.

B. Regulatory Compliance.

C. Cyber-Physical Systems.

D. Virtual Reality.

7. What kind of analytics uses artificial intelligence to provide actionable insights and recommendations?

   A. Descriptive Analytics.

   B. Diagnostic Analytics.

   C. Predictive Analytics.

   D. Augmented Analytics.

8. Which approach to data management focuses on interoperability and real-time processing to support applications that require integration of diverse data sources?

   A. Data Federation.

   B. Data Propagation.

   C. Data Mesh.

   D. Data Fabric.

9. What are systems that are capable of performing tasks that normally require human intelligence, such as speech recognition, decision-making, and translation between languages, called?

   A. Decision Support Systems.

   B. Autonomous Systems.

   C. Artificial Intelligence (AI).

D. Expert Systems.

10. What is the practice of protecting computer systems and information networks from intrusion or unauthorized access?

   A. Data Privacy.

   B. Information Management.

   C. Cybersecurity.

   D. Risk Management.

11. What is natural language processing (NLP) and what is its role in modern business?

   A. A form of distributed computing that facilitates the operation and management of large data sets.

   B. An algorithmic technique for analyzing and interpreting abstract data.

   C. Technology that enables the understanding and generation of human language by computers.

   D. A data visualization method for representing complex information in an understandable manner.

12. What technology trend aims to make Artificial Intelligence more accessible and useful for companies without data specialists?

   A. Automated Machine Learning (AutoML).

   B. In-memory Computing.

C. Quantum Computing.

D. Blockchain.

13. What type of technology is used to create virtual representations of real-world objects or systems to simulate their processes?

A. Virtual Reality (VR).

B. Augmented Reality (AR).

C. Digital Twins.

D. Edge Computing.

14. What technology is behind the ability to process and analyze data at the location where it is collected, rather than sending it to a centralized data center?

A. Fog Computing.

B. Cloud Analytics.

C. Decentralized Data Ecosystem.

D. Edge Computing.

15. What are the gigantic data sets that cannot be processed or analyzed using traditional methods called?

A. Big Data.

B. Thick Data.

C. Smart Data.

D. Heavy Data.

16. What kind of analytics focuses on providing insights into what will happen in the future, based on historical data?

A. Descriptive Analytics.

B. Predictive Analytics.

C. Prescriptive Analytics.

D. Diagnostic Analytics.

17. The trend of decentralizing data where it remains close to the source to reduce latency and improve security is known as what?

A. Data Gravity.

B. Data Proximity.

C. Data Localization.

D. Data Sovereignty.

18. What does the term 'Analytics as a Service' (AaaS) describe?

A. A platform that offers on-premises data analysis tools.

B. A business model where data analytics is offered as a cloud-based service.

C. Software that needs to be installed locally to perform data analysis.

D. Dedicated devices that perform data analysis.

19. Which emerging data analysis technique involves the simultaneous application of multiple machine learning algorithms to optimize predictive performance?

A. Predictive Modelling.

B. Ensemble Learning.

C. Transfer Learning.

D. Deep Learning.

20. What is the term for the area of analytics that focuses on gaining insights from unstructured text through natural language processing and other analytics techniques?

A. Text Analytics.

B. Audio Analytics.

C. Video Analytics.

D. Sentiment Analytics.

21. Which analytical approach is growing in popularity due to its ability to create models that can explain decisions and predict future behaviors?

A. Descriptive Analytics.

B. Cognitive Analytics.

C. Prescriptive Analytics.

D. Diagnostic Analytics.

22. What analytics and data technology do companies focus on to perform analysis of large volumes of data on the go, often to respond in near real-time?

A. Batch Processing.

B. Real-time Analytics.

C. Historical Data Analysis.

D. Periodic Reporting.

23. Which trend in analytics allows you to simulate business scenarios and predict the effects of future decisions before they happen?

A. What-if Analysis.

B. Descriptive Analysis.

C. Diagnostic Analysis.

D. Time-series Analysis.

24. What is the name of the technology of recent existence that uses sophisticated algorithms to automate the preparation and cleansing of data?

    A. Data Scrubbing.

    B. Data Preparation Automation.

    C. ETL (Extract, Transform, Load) Automation.

    D. Data Curation.

25. The use of what devices has grown within the field of analytics to collect large amounts of data in a variety of environments, thus contributing to the Internet of Things?

    A. Smart Sensors.

    B. Smartphones.

    C. Tablets.

    D. Personal Computers.

26. Which technology is essential to enable real-time and interactive Data Visualization?

    A. Data Warehousing.

    B. ETL Tools.

C. Business Intelligence (BI) Platforms.

D. In-memory Data Grids.

27. Which analytics trend involves using graphs to model relationships between complex entities or interrelated data sets?

A. Graph Analytics.

B. Descriptive Analytics.

C. Predictive Analytics.

D. Diagnostic Analytics

28. What is the automated process of using algorithms to fit machine learning models without human intervention called?

A. Model Fitting.

B. Auto-tuning.

C. Hyperparameter Optimization.

D. Automated Model Training.

29. In the context of Big Data, what are the '3 Vs' that characterize the challenges and opportunities?

A. Volume, Velocity, Variety.

B. Vision, Value, Verification.

C. Virtual, Viable, Volatile.

D. Vector, View, Visualization.

30. What does the abbreviation 'NLP' mean in the context of analytics trends?

A. Network Layer Protocol.

B. Natural Learning Process.

C. Nonlinear Programming.

D. Natural Language Processing.

31. What is the term used to describe the analysis of large volumes of data generated from devices connected to the internet?

A. Social Media Analytics.

B. IoT Analytics.

C. Web Analytics.

D. Cloud Analytics.

32. What is the name of the application of advanced analytics techniques that explore texts, images, video and audio?

A. Multimedia Analytics.

B. Unstructured Data Analysis.

C. Content Analytics.

D. Rich Media Analysis.

33. Which technology combines data storage resources and computational resources for efficient and agile Big Data processing?

A. Hybrid Transactional/Analytical Processing (HTAP).

B. Data Lakehouse.

C. NoSQL Databases.

D. Data Warehouse Appliance.

34. Which analytics trend focuses on creating interactive visual models that allow users to understand data intricacies and depths?

A. Predictive Modeling.

B. Interactive Data Visualization.

C. Diagnostic Analytics.

D. Cognitive Analytics.

35. What is the technology that enables the analysis and processing of large geographically dispersed data sets in real time?

A. Distributed Data Storage.

B. Cloud Computing.

C. Edge Computing.

D. Fog Computing.

36. What does "AaaS" mean in modern enterprise analytics trends?

    A. Analytics as a Service.

    B. Algorithms as a Service.

    C. Automation as a Service.

    D. Artificial Intelligence as a Service.

37. What trend in technology facilitates real-time queries on large distributed data sets?

    A. Data Virtualization.

    B. OLTP (Online Transaction Processing).

    C. Real-Time BI (Business Intelligence).

    D. In-Memory Computing.

38. In analytics, what is 'Data Fabric'?

    A. A new programming language for data.

    B. A physical data storage infrastructure.

    C. An integrated environment that uses an architecture and services to support enterprise-wide data capabilities.

    D. A real-time data processing technique.

39. What technology enables companies to identify customer behavior trends by analyzing data at scale?

    A. CRM Analytics.

    B. Consumer Behavior Modeling.

    C. Sentiment Analysis.

    D. Customer Data Platforms (CDP).

40. What is the name of analytics technology where data is processed and analyzed the instant it occurs?

    A. Batch Analytics.

    B. Real-Time Analytics.

    C. Historical Analytics.

    D. Predictive Analytics.

41. What technology trend involves adding an intelligent layer to data governance, which allows data policies to be operationalized dynamically?

    A. Intelligent Data Management.

    B. Automated Data Governance.

    C. Self-Service Data Prep.

    D. Data Ops (Data Operations).

3.2   Answers.

1. C. Big Data Analytics.

2. B. In-memory Analytics.

3. A. A network of physical devices that collect and share electronic data.

4. B. Explainable AI.

5. A. Edge Analytics.

6. B. Regulatory Compliance.

7. D. Augmented Analytics.

8. D. Data Fabric.

9. C. Artificial Intelligence (AI).

10. C. Cybersecurity.

11. C. Technology that enables the understanding and generation of human language by computers.

12. A. Automated Machine Learning (AutoML).

13. C. Digital Twins.

14. D. Edge Computing.

15. A. Big Data.

16. B. Predictive Analytics.

17. C. Data Localization.

18. B. A business model where data analytics is offered as a cloud-based service.

19. B. Ensemble Learning.

20. A. Text Analytics.

21. B. Cognitive Analytics.

22. B. Real-time Analytics.

23. A. What-if Analysis.

24. B. Data Preparation Automation.

25. A. Smart Sensors.

26. C. Business Intelligence (BI) Platforms.

27. A. Graph Analytics.

28. C. Hyperparameter Optimization.

29. A. Volume, Velocity, Variety.

30. D. Natural Language Processing.

31. B. IoT Analytics.

32. C. Content Analytics.

33. A. Hybrid Transactional/Analytical Processing (HTAP).

34. B. Interactive Data Visualization.

35. C. Edge Computing.

36. A. Analytics as a Service.

37. A. Data Virtualization.

38. C. An integrated environment that uses an architecture and services to support enterprise-wide data capabilities.

39. D. Customer Data Platforms (CDP).

40. B. Real-Time Analytics.

41. A. Intelligent Data Management.

4 Augmented Analytics.

4.1 Questions.

1. What is Augmented Analytics?

    A. A technology that focuses exclusively on increasing the speed of data processing.

    B. An advanced analytics approach that uses artificial intelligence to improve data preparation and insight discovery.

    C. A virtual reality tool applied to the field of business intelligence (BI).

    D. An analysis method that relies entirely on manual data analysis.

2. How does Augmented Analytics benefit data scientists?

    A. Automating routine tasks and allowing them to focus on more complex analyses.

    B. Removing the need for any human interaction with data.

    C. Replacing the need for data scientists in organizations.

    D. Increasing the complexity of the data to test your skills.

3. Which Augmented Analytics capability is critical to generating insights from large volumes of data?

    A. Manual Data Processing.

    B. Machine Learning.

C. Cloud Storage.

D. Simple Sorting Algorithms.

4. What is the main objective of Augmented Analytics in the business context?

    A. Decrease transparency and increase data centralization.

    B. Facilitate decision-making based on managerial intuition.

    C. Enable organizations to make data-driven decisions faster and more accurately.

    D. Increase the need for IT specialists to handle analytical tools.

5. What does NLP (Natural Language Processing) enable in Augmented Analytics?

    A. Data migration across different platforms.

    B. Data analysis using natural language to generate reports and visualizations.

    C. Connecting IoT devices to receive real-time data.

    D. Creation of security modules to block cyber intrusions.

6. What capabilities are enhanced by Augmented Analytics in Business Intelligence (BI) tools?

    A. Transaction Processing and Data Storage.

B. Data preparation, insight generation, and data visualization.

C. Hardware capabilities and server response time.

D. Cybersecurity and data protection algorithms.

7. What role of Augmented Analytics allows lay users to perform complex analysis?

A. Complex programming interface (API).

B. Natural Language Generation (NLG).

C. Static charts and basic dashboards.

D. Advanced regression models.

8. How does Augmented Analytics help democratize data within an organization?

A. Restricting access to data to a given set of analysis tools.

B. Developing an advanced technical understanding in all employees.

C. Making data access and understanding more accessible to non-experts through automation and user-friendly interfaces.

D. Increasing reliance on IT teams to generate analytical reports.

9. Which of these is a practical application of Augmented Analytics in a business environment?

   A. Automate the data entry process.

   B. Make predictions and provide recommendations for action.

   C. Replace human decision-making in all instances.

   D. Minimize the use of any type of data visualization.

10. What kind of technologies does augmented analytics employ to enhance analytics?

    A. Relational Database Technologies Exclusively.

    B. Machine Learning and Natural Language Processing.

    C. Satellite connections for data transmission.

    D. Simple neural networks for arithmetic operations.

4.2   Answers.

1. B. An advanced analytics approach that uses artificial intelligence to improve data preparation and insight discovery.

2. A. Automating routine tasks and allowing them to focus on more complex analyses.

3. B. Machine Learning.

4. C. Enable organizations to make data-driven decisions faster and more accurately.

5. B. Data analysis using natural language to generate reports and visualizations.

6. B. Data preparation, insight generation, and data visualization.

7. B. Natural Language Generation (NLG).

8. C. Making data access and understanding more accessible to non-experts through automation and user-friendly interfaces.

9. B. Make predictions and provide recommendations for action.

10. B. Machine Learning and Natural Language Processing.

5 Continuous Intelligence.

5.1 Questions.

1. What is Continuous Intelligence?

   A. A batch data processing technique that occurs at regular intervals.

   B. A Business Intelligence practice that relies solely on monthly static reports.

   C. An analytical approach that integrates real-time data processing with advanced machine learning techniques for continuous insights.

   D. A data backup system that updates information in real-time.

2. What is the main benefit of Continuous Intelligence for organizations?

   A. Reduces the amount of data required for effective analysis.

   B. Eliminates the need for data analysis by professionals.

   C. Improves the speed and accuracy of decisions based on the latest available data.

   D. Increases the complexity of reports for maximum detail.

3. What technologies is Continuous Intelligence strongly based on?

   A. Traditional Business Intelligence and Data Warehousing.

   B. Machine Learning, Big Data and Cloud Computing.

   C. Mainframes and batch processing.

   D. Relational databases and magnetic data storage.

4. How can Continuous Intelligence be applied to customer service?

   A. Using historical data exclusively to understand past behavior patterns.

   B. Through automatic interactions and pre-defined scripts based on decision trees.

   C. Analyzing real-time interaction data to personalize and improve the customer experience.

   D. Limiting customer communication based on weekly data insights.

5. Which characteristic is essential for the effective implementation of Continuous Intelligence in an organization?

   A. A rigid hierarchical organizational structure that centralizes decision-making.

   B. Static data storage technologies that are updated quarterly.

C. Dispersed computational capacity that makes it difficult to access current data immediately.

D. Technological infrastructure that supports the rapid analysis and integration of different data sources.

6. What differentiates Continuous Intelligence from traditional Business Intelligence (BI) approaches?

    A. The exclusive reliance on historical data sets.

    B. The ability to provide static insights based on periodic reports.

    C. The use of real-time predictive and prescriptive analytics.

    D. The absence of Machine Learning technology in data analysis.

7. What is the most critical component for a Continuous Intelligence infrastructure?

    A. Legacy data storage systems.

    B. Powerful real-time processing systems.

    C. Detailed analysis procedure manuals.

    D. Static databases for long-term storage.

8. What are the main benefits of Continuous Intelligence for business operations?

    A. Increased bureaucracy and reduced autonomy in the decision-making process.

B. More agile decisions and anticipation of changes in the market or consumer behavior.

C. Increased reliance on historical data and annual financial reports.

D. Reduction in the volume of data required for analysis.

9. How does Continuous Intelligence relate to emerging data and analytics trends?

A. It is aligned with trends such as Big Data and real-time analytics.

B. It contrasts with the migration to cloud computing and distributed processing.

C. Avoids the use of Machine Learning and Artificial Intelligence technologies.

D. Prefers manual methods of data processing over automated procedures.

10. Which technology is critical to running Continuous Intelligence at enterprise scale?

A. Simple database management software.

B. Electronic spreadsheets and static graphs.

C. Online Transaction Processing Systems (OLTP).

D. Data and analytics platforms that support rapid processing and event-driven decision-making.

11. What is Explainable Artificial Intelligence (XAI)?

a) A form of AI that mimics human intuition.

b) An AI initiative to make its decisions understandable by humans.

c) A new machine learning algorithm.

d) A technique that focuses exclusively on increasing the performance of AI models.

12. Why is explainability important in AI systems?

a) Because systems need to operate independently of humans.

b) To ensure that AI systems can improve their performance without human help.

c) To comply with legal regulations and allow users to trust AI decisions.

d) To make AI programming more complex and advanced.

13. Which of the following is a method used to promote explainability in AI?

a) Data obfuscation.

b) Black-box techniques.

c) Deep Learning.

d) Data visualization techniques.

14. What are "black box" methods in AI?

(a) AI systems whose internal processes are transparent and easily understood.

b) Systems that can explain their own decisions without any human intervention.

c) Systems in which decision-making processes are opaque and not easily interpretable.

d) Methods that deliberately conceal the inner workings of trade secrets.

15. What does the acronym LIME refer to in Explainable AI?

a) Local Interpretable Model-agnostic Explanations.

b) Linear Interpolation Model for Explanation.

c) Local Integrated Machine Evaluation.

d) Lightweight Interpretive Model Engine.

16. What is the main purpose of Explainable Artificial Intelligence (XAI)?

a) Reduce the cost of producing artificial intelligence models.

b) Make the decision-making process of AI algorithms understandable to humans.

c) Increase the processing speed of AI algorithms.

(d) Integrate AI with other emerging technologies.

17. How do "black box" methods impact explainability in AI?

(a) facilitate the interpretation of the AI's results.

b) obscure the understanding of AI's internal decision-making mechanisms.

c) Provide a step-by-step explanation of the decisions made.

d) They emphasize the complete transparency of the algorithm.

18. What are "post-processing" techniques in XAI?

a) Methods applied during the model training phase.

b) techniques requiring access to the internal AI model.

c) Approaches that modify the AI model to be more explainable after training.

d) Methods that are applied before the development of the model.

19. Which of the following is a benefit of Explainable Artificial Intelligence?

a) Reduction of the need for data storage.

b) Increased complexity of models.

c) Better user acceptance and trust in AI systems.

d) Reduction of machine learning capabilities.

20. What role does "transparency" play in Explainable Artificial Intelligence?

a) Reduce the need for human intervention.

b) Raise the level of safety of AI algorithms.

c) make AI decision-making processes clear and understandable.

d) Simplify the code of artificial intelligence algorithms.

5.2   Answers.

1. C. An analytical approach that integrates real-time data processing with advanced machine learning techniques for continuous insights.

2. C. Improves the speed and accuracy of decisions based on the latest available data.

3. B. Machine Learning, Big Data and Cloud Computing.

4. C. Analyzing real-time interaction data to personalize and improve the customer experience.

5. D. Technological infrastructure that supports the rapid analysis and integration of different data sources.

6. C. The use of real-time predictive and prescriptive analytics.

7. B. Powerful real-time processing systems.

8. B. More agile decisions and anticipation of changes in the market or consumer behavior.

9. A. It is aligned with trends such as Big Data and real-time analytics.

10. D. Data and analytics platforms that support rapid processing and event-driven decision-making.

11. b) An AI initiative to make its decisions understandable by humans.

12. c) To comply with legal regulations and allow users to trust AI

decisions.

13. d) Data visualization techniques.

14. c) Systems in which decision-making processes are opaque and not easily interpretable.

15. a) Local Interpretable Model-agnostic Explanations.

16. b) Make the decision-making process of AI algorithms understandable to humans.

17. b) obscure the understanding of AI's internal decision-making mechanisms.

18. c) Approaches that modify the AI model to be more explainable after training.

19. c) Better user acceptance and trust in AI systems.

20. c) make AI decision-making processes clear and understandable.

6 Distributed computing.

6.1 Questions.

1. What is distributed computing in Big Data?

   a) A technique for storing large amounts of data on a single server.

   b) A process of distributing large data sets across multiple physical locations.

   c) A computing system where many components located in different systems work together.

   d) A method of data backup where copies are stored in multiple locations.

2. What is the main benefit of distributed computing in Big Data?

   a) Reduce the need for data specialists.

   b) Increase data security through obscurity.

   c) Enable parallel processing that can significantly improve performance.

   d) Decrease the cost of hardware components due to lower demand.

3. Why is fault tolerance important in distributed big data computing?

   a) Because it guarantees that the system will never fail.

b) Allows the system to operate continuously even when some components fail.

c) Because it helps to distribute the data more evenly.

d) Makes data backup obsolete.

4. What consistency model is often used in distributed big data computing to manage data updates?

a) Strong consistency.

b) Eventual consistency.

c) Immediate consistency.

d) Linear consistency.

5. What is distributed computing in Big Data?

a) A technique for storing large amounts of data on a single server.

b) A process of distributing large data sets across multiple physical locations.

c) A computing system where many components located in different systems work together.

d) A method of data backup where copies are stored in multiple locations.

6. What is the main benefit of distributed computing in Big Data?

    a) Reduce the need for data specialists.

    b) Increase data security through obscurity.

    c) Enable parallel processing that can significantly improve performance.

    d) Decrease the cost of hardware components due to lower demand.

7. Why is fault tolerance important in distributed big data computing?

    a) Because it guarantees that the system will never fail.

    b) Allows the system to operate continuously even when some components fail.

    c) Because it helps to distribute the data more evenly.

    d) Makes data backup obsolete.

8. What consistency model is often used in distributed big data computing to manage data updates?

    a) Strong consistency.

    b) Eventual consistency.

    c) Immediate consistency.

    d) Linear consistency.

9. What defines the term "Sharding" in distributed computing?

   a) The technique of creating replicas of data on different servers.

   b) The encryption of data before it is distributed.

   c) The process of dividing and distributing data across multiple nodes of a network.

   d) Reducing the size of the dataset to fit limited computational resources.

10. How does MapReduce make it easy to process big data in a distributed computing environment?

    a) Concentrating computing in a single powerful processing core.

    b) Reducing the need for processing through the elimination of excessive data.

    c) Dividing tasks into small parts and processing them in parallel in different nodes.

    d) Using a single powerful server to quickly process large volume of data.

11. What role does Apache Hadoop play in the context of Big Data?

    a) Serve as a primary tool for data visualization.

    b) Operate as a relational database management system.

    c) Function as a platform that supports distributed data processing.

d) Act as a user interface to simplify access to NoSQL databases.

12. What does the 'Lambda Architecture' model consist of in Big Data processing?

a) Complete separation of batch and real-time processing systems.

b) An architecture that emphasizes data processing exclusively in real time.

c) A mix of batch and real-time processing to take advantage of both.

d) The use of a single processing layer that scales between batch and real time.

13. What is the importance of 'Data Governance' in the field of Big Data?

a) Reduce the amount of data to be processed.

b) Establish rules and policies to manage and protect data.

c) Completely automate the data analysis process.

d) Emphasize the use of unstructured data over structured data.

6.2   Answers.

1. c) A computing system where many components located in different systems work together.

2. c) Enable parallel processing that can significantly improve performance.

3. b) Allows the system to operate continuously even when some components fail.

4. b) Eventual consistency.

5. c) A computing system where many components located in different systems work together.

6. c) Enable parallel processing that can significantly improve performance.

7. b) Allows the system to operate continuously even when some components fail.

8. b) Eventual consistency.

9. c) The process of dividing and distributing data across multiple nodes of a network.

10. c) Dividing tasks into small parts and processing them in parallel in different nodes.

11. c) Function as a platform that supports distributed data processing.

12. c) A mix of batch and real-time processing to take advantage of both.

13. b) Establish rules and policies to manage and protect data.

7 Latency.

7.1 Questions.

1. In Big Data analytics, what does the term "latency" mean?

   a) The amount of data that can be processed in a given period of time.

   b) The speed with which data is created from its sources.

   c) The time it takes for data to be moved from one point to another.

   d) The delay between data collection and the availability of these data for analysis.

2. How does low latency affect real-time processing in big data?

   a) It makes processing less reliable.

   b) Increases the time needed to perform complex analyses.

   c) Improves the efficiency of responding to data events almost instantaneously.

   d) It has no significant impact on data processing.

3. What is network latency in the context of Big Data?

   a) The efficiency with which the server processes large volumes of data.

   b) The resistance of a network node to accept new connections.

   c) the time required to establish a new network connection.

d) The time it takes for a data packet to travel from its point of origin to its destination.

4. In the context of databases, how does write latency differ from read latency?

a) Write latency refers to the time to retrieve data, while read latency refers to the time to save data.

b) Read and write latency are essentially the same thing in databases.

c) Write latency is the time it takes to write data to the database, while read latency is the time to retrieve that data.

d) Write latency has to do with the deletion of data, read latency with its update.

7.2   Answers.

1. d) The delay between data collection and the availability of these data for analysis.

2. c) Improves the efficiency of responding to data events almost instantaneously.

3. d) The time it takes for a data packet to travel from its point of origin to its destination.

4. c) Write latency is the time it takes to write data to the database, while read latency is the time to retrieve that data.

8 Conclusion.

Throughout this book, we explore the key concepts, challenges, and opportunities provided by Big Data, demonstrating how this technology has revolutionized disparate industries and driven data-driven decision-making.

We discuss how the combination of large volumes of information and sophisticated algorithms not only transforms business models but also redefines the way we interact with the digital and physical worlds.

This book is part of the "700 Big Data Questions" collection, a comprehensive work that has been carefully structured to provide a progressive and in-depth understanding of the various aspects of Big Data.

The five volumes that make up this collection address, in a sequential and complementary way, the fundamental pillars to master this technology:

- Volume 1: Introduces the fundamental concepts of Big Data, exploring its nature as an essential raw material for the new digital economy and its main applications.

- Volume 2: Deepens the understanding of Big Data in the context of information science, analyzing emerging trends, augmented analytics, continuous intelligence, and distributed computing.

- Volume 3: Explores the technological and management aspects of Big Data, including data mining, classification and regression algorithms, and the new professions driven by the advancement of data.

- Volume 4: Addresses the requirements for efficient management of Big Data, including data structures, architecture layers, storage, and the role of Business Intelligence in this ecosystem.

- Volume 5: Focuses on the practical implementation of Big Data, discussing SAAS, IAAS and PAAS, operational costs, challenges for small businesses, digital security and the evolution of the Data Warehouse.

Each volume of this collection is part of the broader project of the Big Data collection, which seeks to consolidate knowledge about the main approaches, tools, and strategies in the management and application of data in the context of Artificial Intelligence. If you want to expand your understanding of these topics and deepen your knowledge in a structured and progressive way, I invite you to explore the other volumes of this series.

The future is driven by data, and those who master this language are at the forefront of innovation. The "700 Big Data Questions" collection is an essential guide for professionals, researchers, and enthusiasts who want to prepare for this new digital era, providing valuable insights and applicable practices in various scenarios.

9 Bibliography.

ACQUISTI, A., BRANDIMARTE, L., & LOEWENSTEIN, G. (2015). Privacy and human behavior in the age of information. Science, 347(6221), 509-514. Available at: https://www.heinz.cmu.edu/~acquisti/papers/Acquisti-Science-Privacy-Review.pdf.

ACQUISTI, A., TAYLOR, C., & WAGMAN, L. (2016). The economics of privacy. Journal of Economic Literature, 54(2), 442-92.

AKIDAU, Tyler, CHERNYAK, Slava, LAX, Reuven. (2019). Streaming Systems: The What, Where, When, and How of Large-Scale Data Processing.

ALGORITHMWATCH. (2019) Automating Society 2019. Available at: https://algorithmwatch.org/en/automating-society-2019/

ARMSTRONG, M. (2006). Competition in two-sided markets. The RAND Journal of Economics.

ARMSTRONG, M. (2006). Competition in two-sided markets. The RAND Journal of Economics, 37(3), 668-691.

BELKIN, N.J. (1978). Information concepts for information science. Journal of Documentation, v. 34, n. 1, p. 55-85.

BOLLIER, D., & Firestone, C. M. (2010). The promise and peril of Big Data. Washington, DC: Aspen Institute, Communications and Society Program.

BOYD, D; CRAWFORD, K. (2012). Critical Questions for Big Data: Provocations for a Cultural, Technological, and Scholarly Phenomenon. Information, Communication, & Society v.15, n.5, p. 662-679.

BRETON, P. & PROULX S. (1989). L'explosion de la communication. la naissance d'une nouvelle idéologie. Paris: La Découverte.

BUBENKO, J. A., WANGLER, B. (1993). "Objectives Driven Capture of Business Rules and of Information System Requirements". IEEE Systems Man and Cybernetics'93 Conference, Le Touquet, France.

CHEN, H., CHIANG, R. H., & STOREY, V. C. (2012). Business Intelligence and Analytics: From Big Data to Big Impact. MIS Quarterly.

CHENG, Y., Qin, C., & RUSU, F. (2012). Big Data Analytics made easy. SIGMOD '12 Proceedings of the 2012 ACM SIGMOD International Conference on Management of Data New York.

COHEN, Reuven. (2012). Brazil's Booming Business of Big Data – Available at: https://www.forbes.com/sites/reuvencohen/2012/12/12/brazil s-booming-business-of-bigdata/?sh=1de7e6bc4682

COMPUTERWORLD. (2016) Ten cases of Big Data that guaranteed a significant return on investment. Available at: https://computerworld.com.br/plataformas/10-casos-de-big-data-que-garantiram-expressivo-retorno-sobre-investimento/.

DAVENPORT, T. H. (2014). Big Data at work: debunking myths and uncovering opportunities. Rio de Janeiro: Elsevier.

DAVENPORT, T; PATIL, D. (2012). Data scientist: the sexiest job of the 21st century. Harvard Business Review. Available at: https://hbr.org/2012/10/data-scientist-the-sexiest-job-of-the-21st-century.

DAVENPORT, T; PATIL, D. (2012). Data scientist: the sexiest job of the 21st century. Harvard Business Review. Available at: https://hbr.org/2012/10/data-scientist-the-sexiest-job-of-the-21st-century.

DIXON, James. 2010. Pentaho, Hadoop, and Data Lakes. Blog, October. Available   at: https://jamesdixon.wordpress.com/2010/10/14/pentaho-hadoop-and-data-lakes/

EDWARD Choi, M. T. (2017). RETAIN: An Interpretable Predictive Model for Healthcare using Reverse Time Attention Mechanism. Available in https://arxiv.org/pdf/1608.05745.pdf

GLASS, R. ; CALLAHAN, (2015).S. The Big Data-Driven Business: How to Use Big Data to Win Customers, Beat Competitors, and Boost Profit. New Jersey: John Wiley & Sons, Inc.

GÓMEZ-BARROSO, J. L. (2018). Experiments on personal information disclosure: Past and future avenues. Telematics and Informatics, 35(5),   1473-1490.Available   at: https://doi.org/10.1016/j.tele.2018.03.017

GUALTIERI, M. (2013). Big Data Predictive Analytics Solutions. Massachusetts: Forrester.

HALPER, F. (2013). How To Gain Insight From Text. TDWI Checklist Report.

HALPER, F., & KRISHNAN, K. (2013). TDWI Big Data Maturity Model Guide Interpreting Your Assessment Score. TDWI Benchmark Guide 2013–2014.

HELBING, D. (2014). The World after Big Data: What the Digital Revolution Means for Us. Available at: http://papers.ssrn.com/sol3/papers.cfm?abstract_id=2438957.

HELBING, D. (2015a). Big Data Society: Age of Reputation or Age of Discrimination?. In: HELBING, D. Thinking Ahead-Essays on Big Data, Digital Revolution, and Participatory Market Society. Springer International Publishing. p. 103-114.

HELBING, D. (2015b). Thinking Ahead-Essays on Big Data, Digital Revolution, and Participatory Market Society. Springer International Publishing.

HILBERT, M. (2013). Big Data for Development: From Information to Knowledge Societies. Available at https://www.researchgate.net/publication/254950835_Big_Dat a_for_Development_From_Information-_to_Knowledge_Societies.

IBM. (2014). Exploiting Big Data in telecommunications to increase revenue, reduce customer churn and operating costs. Source: IBM: http://www-01.ibm.com/software/data/bigdata/industry-telco.html.

INMON, W. H. (1992). Building the Data Warehouse. John Wiley & Sons, New York, NY, USA.

INMON, W. H. (1996). Building the Data Warehouse. John Wiley & Sons, New Yorkm NY, USA.2nd edition.

JARVELIN, K. & Vakkari, P. (1993) The evolution of Library and Information Science 1965-1985: a content analysis of journal articles. Information Processing & Management, v.29, n.1, p. 129-144.

KAMIOKA, T; TAPANAINEN, T. (2014). Organizational use of Big Data and competitive advantage - Exploration of Antecedents. Available at: https://www.researchgate.net/publication/284551664_Organiz ational_Use_of_Big_Data_and_Competitive_Advantage_-_Exploration_of_Antecedents.

KANDALKAR, N.A; WADHE, A. (2014). Extracting Large Data using Big Data Mining, International Journal of Engineering Trends and Technology. v. 9, n.11, p.576-582.

KIMBALL, R.; ROSS, M. (2013). The Data Warehouse Toolkit: The Definitive Guide to Dimensional Modeling, Third Edition. Wiley 10475 Crosspoint Boulevard Indianapolis, IN 46256: John Wiley & Sons, Inc.

KSHETRI, N. (2014). Big Data' s impact on privacy, security and consumer welfare. Telecommunications Policy, 38(11), 1134-1145.

LAVALLE, S., LESSER, E., SHOCKLEY, R., HOPKINS, M. S., & KRUSCHWITZ, N. (2010). Big Data, Analytics and the Path From Insights to Value.

LOHR, S. (2012). The Age of Big Data. The New York Times.

MACHADO, Felipe Nery Rodrigues. 2018. Database-Design and Implementation. [S.l.]: Editora Saraiva.

MANYIKA, J., CHUI, M., BROWN, B., BUGHIN, J., DOBBS, R., ROXBURGH, C., & BYERS, A. H. (2011). Big Data: The next frontier for innovation, competition, and productivity.

OHLHORST, J. F. (2012). Big Data Analytics: Turning Big Data into Big Money. Wiley.

OSWALDO, T., PJOTR, P., MARC, S., & RITSERT, C. J. (2011). Big Data, but are we ready? Available at: https://www.nature.com/articles/nrg2857-c1.

PAVLO, A., PAULSON, E., RASIN, A., ABADI, D. J., DEWITT, D. J., MADDEN, S., & STONEBRAKER, M. (2009). A comparison of approaches to large-scale data analysis. SIGMOD, pp. 165–178.

RAJ, P., & DEKA, G. C. (2012). Handbook of Research on Cloud Infrastructures for Big Data Analytics. Information Science: IGI Global.

SUBRAMANIAM, Anushree. 2020. What is Big Data? – A Beginner's Guide to the World of Big Data. Available at: edureka.co/blog/what-is-big-data/.

TANKARD, C. (2012). Big Data security, Network Security, Volume 2012, Issue7, July 2012, Pages 5 -8, ISSN 1353-4858.

TM FORUM. (2005). SLA management handbook - volume 2. Technical Report GB9712, TeleManagement Forum.

VAISHNAVI, V. K., & KUECHLER, W. (2004). Design Science Research in Information Systems.

VAN AALST, W. M., VAN HEE, K. M., VAN WERF, J. M., & VERDONK, M. (March 2010). Auditing 2.0: Using Process Mining to Support Tomorrow's Auditor. Computer (Volume:43, Issue:3.

WANG, Y., KUNG, L., & BYRD, T. A. (2018). Big Data analytics: Understanding its capabilities and potential benefits for healthcare organizations. Technological Forecasting and Social Change, 126, 3-13.

WIDJAYA, Ivan. (2019). What are the costs of big data? Available at: http://www.smbceo.com/2019/09/04/what-are-the-costs-of-big-data/

10 Big Data Collection: Unlocking the Future of Data in an Essential Collection.

The *Big Data* collection was created to be an indispensable guide for professionals, students, and enthusiasts who want to confidently navigate the vast and fascinating universe of data. In an increasingly digital and interconnected world, Big Data is not just a tool, but a fundamental strategy for the transformation of businesses, processes, and decisions. This collection sets out to simplify complex concepts and empower your readers to turn data into valuable insights.

Each volume in the collection addresses an essential component of this area, combining theory and practice to offer a broad and integrated understanding. You'll find themes such as:

In addition to exploring the fundamentals, the collection also looks into the future, with discussions on emerging trends such as the integration of artificial intelligence, text analytics, and governance in increasingly dynamic and global environments.

Whether you're a manager looking for ways to optimize processes, a data scientist exploring new techniques, or a beginner curious to understand the impact of data on everyday life, the *Big Data* collection is the ideal partner on this journey. Each book has been developed with accessible yet technically sound language, allowing readers of all levels to advance their understanding and skills.

Get ready to master the power of data and stand out in an ever-evolving market. The *Big Data* collection is available on Amazon and is the key to unlocking the future of data-driven intelligence.

10.1   Who is the Big Data collection for.

The *Big Data* collection is designed to cater to a diverse audience that shares the goal of understanding and applying the power of data in an increasingly information-driven world. Whether you're a seasoned professional or just starting your journey in the technology and data space, this collection offers valuable insights, practical examples, and indispensable tools.

1. Technology and Data Professionals.

Data scientists, data engineers, analysts, and developers will find in the collection the fundamentals they need to master concepts such as Big Data Analytics, distributed computing, Hadoop, and advanced tools. Each volume covers technical topics in a practical way, with clear explanations and examples that can be applied in everyday life.

2. Managers and Organizational Leaders.

For leaders and managers, the collection offers a strategic view on how to implement and manage Big Data projects. The books show how to use data to optimize processes, identify opportunities, and make informed decisions. Real-world examples illustrate how companies have used Big Data to transform their businesses in industries such as retail, healthcare, and the environment.

3. Entrepreneurs and Small Businesses.

Entrepreneurs and small business owners who want to leverage the power of data to improve their competitiveness can also benefit. The collection presents practical strategies for using Big Data in a scalable way, demystifying the idea that this technology is exclusive to large corporations.

4. Students and Beginners in the Area.

If you're a student or just starting to explore the universe of Big Data, this collection is the perfect starting point. With accessible language and practical examples, the books make complex concepts more understandable, preparing you to dive deeper into data science and artificial intelligence.

5. Curious and Technology Enthusiasts.

For those who, even outside of the corporate or academic environment, have an interest in understanding how Big Data is shaping the world, the collection offers a fascinating and educational introduction. Discover how data is transforming areas as diverse as health, sustainability, and human behavior.

Regardless of your level of expertise or the industry you're in, the *Big Data* collection is designed to empower your readers with actionable insights, emerging trends, and a comprehensive view of the future of data. If you're looking to understand and apply the power of Big Data to grow professionally or transform your business, this collection is for you. Available on Amazon, it is the essential guide to mastering the impact of data in the digital age.

10.2   Get to know the books in the Collection.

10.2.1 Simplifying Big Data into 7 Chapters.

This book is an essential guide for anyone who wants to understand and apply the fundamental concepts of Big Data in a clear and practical way. In a straightforward and accessible format, the book covers everything from theoretical pillars, such as the 5 Vs of Big Data, to modern tools and techniques, including Hadoop and Big Data Analytics.

Exploring real examples and strategies applicable in areas such as health, retail, and the environment, this work is ideal for technology professionals, managers, entrepreneurs, and students looking to transform data into valuable insights.

With an approach that connects theory and practice, this book is the perfect starting point for mastering the Big Data universe and leveraging its possibilities.

10.2.2 Big Data Management.

This book offers a practical and comprehensive approach to serving a diverse audience, from beginner analysts to experienced managers, students, and entrepreneurs.

With a focus on the efficient management of large volumes of information, this book presents in-depth analysis, real-world examples, comparisons between technologies such as Hadoop and Apache Spark, and practical strategies to avoid pitfalls and drive success.

Each chapter is structured to provide applicable insights, from the fundamentals to advanced analytics tools.

10.2.3 Big Data Architecture.

This book is intended for a diverse audience, including data architects who need to build robust platforms, analysts who want to understand how data layers integrate, and executives who are looking to inform informed decisions. Students and researchers in computer science, data engineering, and management will also find here a solid and up-to-date reference.

The content combines a practical approach and conceptual rigor. You'll be guided from the fundamentals, such as the 5 Vs of Big Data, to the complexity of layered architectures, spanning infrastructure, security, analytics tools, and storage standards like Data Lake and Data Warehouse. In addition, clear examples, real case studies, and technology comparisons will help turn theoretical knowledge into practical applications and effective strategies.

10.2.4 Big Data Implementation.

This volume has been carefully crafted to be a practical and accessible guide, connecting theory to practice for professionals and students who want to master the strategic implementation of Big Data solutions.

It covers everything from quality analysis and data integration to topics such as real-time processing, virtualization, security, and governance, offering clear and applicable examples.

10.2.5 Strategies to Reduce Costs and Maximize Big Data Investments.

With a practical and reasoned approach, this book offers detailed analysis, real case studies and strategic solutions for IT managers, data analysts, entrepreneurs and business professionals.

This book is an indispensable guide to understanding and optimizing the costs associated with implementing Big Data, covering everything from storage and processing to small business-specific strategies and cloud cost analysis.

As part of the "Big Data" collection, it connects to other volumes that deeply explore the technical and strategic dimensions of the field, forming an essential library for anyone seeking to master the challenges and opportunities of the digital age.

10.2.6 700 Big Data Questions Collection.

This collection is designed to provide dynamic, challenging, and hands-on learning. With 700 questions strategically crafted and distributed in 5 volumes, it allows you to advance in the domain of Big Data in a progressive and engaging way. Each answer is an opportunity to expand your vision and apply concepts realistically and effectively.

The collection consists of the following books:

1   BIG DATA: 700 Questions - Volume 1.

It deals with information as the raw material for everything, the fundamental concepts and applications of Big Data.

2   BIG DATA: 700 Questions - Volume 2.

It addresses Big Data in the context of information science, data technology trends and analytics, Augmented analytics, continuous intelligence, distributed computing, and latency.

3   BIG DATA: 700 Questions - Volume 3.

It conAnswerss the technological and management aspects of Big Data, data mining, classification trees, logistic regression and professions in the context of Big Data.

4   BIG DATA: 700 Questions - Volume 4.

It deals with the requirements for Big Data management, the data structures used, the architecture and storage layers, Business Intelligence in the context of Big Data, and application virtualization.

5   BIG DATA: 700 Questions - Volume 5.

The book deals with SAAS, IAAS AND PAAS, Big Data implementation, overhead and hidden costs, Big Data for small businesses, digital security and data warehousing in the context of Big Data.

10.2.7 Big Data Glossary.

As large-scale data becomes the heart of strategic decisions in a variety of industries, this book offers a bridge between technical jargon and practical clarity, allowing you to turn complex information into valuable insights.

With clear definitions, practical examples, and intuitive organization, this glossary is designed to cater to a wide range of readers – from developers and data engineers to managers and the curious looking to explore the transformative impact of Big Data in their fields.

11 Discover the "Artificial Intelligence and the Power of Data" Collection – An Invitation to Transform Your Career and Knowledge.

The "Artificial Intelligence and the Power of Data" Collection was created for those who want not only to understand Artificial Intelligence (AI), but also to apply it strategically and practically.

In a series of carefully crafted volumes, I unravel complex concepts in a clear and accessible manner, ensuring the reader has a thorough understanding of AI and its impact on modern societies.

No matter what your level of familiarity with the topic, this collection turns the difficult into the didactic, the theoretical into the applicable, and the technical into something powerful for your career.

11.1 Why buy this collection?

We are living through an unprecedented technological revolution, where AI is the driving force in areas such as medicine, finance, education, government, and entertainment.

The collection "Artificial Intelligence and the Power of Data" dives deep into all these sectors, with practical examples and reflections that go far beyond traditional concepts.

You'll find both the technical expertise and the ethical and social implications of AI encouraging you to see this technology not just as a tool, but as a true agent of transformation.

Each volume is a fundamental piece of this innovative puzzle: from machine learning to data governance and from ethics to practical application.

With the guidance of an experienced author who combines academic research with years of hands-on practice, this collection is more than a set of books – it's an indispensable guide for anyone looking to navigate and excel in this burgeoning field.

11.2   Target Audience of this Collection?

This collection is for everyone who wants to play a prominent role in the age of AI:

- ✓ Tech Professionals: Receive deep technical insights to expand their skills.

- ✓ Students and the Curious: have access to clear explanations that facilitate the understanding of the complex universe of AI.

- ✓ Managers, business leaders, and policymakers will also benefit from the strategic vision on AI, which is essential for making well-informed decisions.

- ✓ Professionals in Career Transition: Professionals in career transition or interested in specializing in AI will find here complete material to build their learning trajectory.

11.3   Much More Than Technique – A Complete Transformation.

This collection is not just a series of technical books; It is a tool for intellectual and professional growth.

With it, you go far beyond theory: each volume invites you to a deep reflection on the future of humanity in a world where machines and algorithms are increasingly present.

This is your invitation to master the knowledge that will define the future and become part of the transformation that Artificial Intelligence brings to the world.

Be a leader in your industry, master the skills the market demands, and prepare for the future with the "Artificial Intelligence and the Power of Data" collection.

This is not just a purchase; It is a decisive investment in your learning and professional development journey.

12 The Books of the Collection.

12.1   Data, Information and Knowledge in the era of Artificial Intelligence.

This book essentially explores the theoretical and practical foundations of Artificial Intelligence, from data collection to its transformation into intelligence. It focuses primarily on machine learning, AI training, and neural networks.

12.2   From Data to Gold: How to Turn Information into Wisdom in the Age of AI.

This book offers critical analysis on the evolution of Artificial Intelligence, from raw data to the creation of artificial wisdom, integrating neural networks, deep learning, and knowledge modeling.

It presents practical examples in health, finance, and education, and addresses ethical and technical challenges.

12.3   Challenges and Limitations of Data in AI.

The book offers an in-depth analysis of the role of data in the development of AI exploring topics such as quality, bias, privacy, security, and scalability with practical case studies in healthcare, finance, and public safety.

12.4   Historical Data in Databases for AI: Structures, Preservation, and Purge.

This book investigates how historical data management is essential to the success of AI projects. It addresses the relevance of ISO standards to ensure quality and safety, in addition to analyzing trends and innovations in data processing.

12.5   Controlled Vocabulary for Data Dictionary: A Complete Guide.

This comprehensive guide explores the advantages and challenges of implementing controlled vocabularies in the context of AI and information science. With a detailed approach, it covers everything from the naming of data elements to the interactions between semantics and cognition.

12.6   Data Curation and Management for the Age of AI.

This book presents advanced strategies for transforming raw data into valuable insights, with a focus on meticulous curation and efficient data management. In addition to technical solutions, it addresses ethical and legal issues, empowering the reader to face the complex challenges of information.

12.7   Information Architecture.

The book addresses data management in the digital age, combining theory and practice to create efficient and scalable AI systems, with insights into modeling and ethical and legal challenges.

12.8   Fundamentals: The Essentials of Mastering Artificial Intelligence.

An essential work for anyone who wants to master the key concepts of AI, with an accessible approach and practical examples. The book explores innovations such as Machine Learning and Natural Language

Processing, as well as ethical and legal challenges, and offers a clear view of the impact of AI on various industries.

12.9   LLMS - Large-Scale Language Models.

This essential guide helps you understand the revolution of Large-Scale Language Models (LLMs) in AI.

The book explores the evolution of GPTs and the latest innovations in human-computer interaction, offering practical insights into their impact on industries such as healthcare, education, and finance.

12.10   Machine Learning: Fundamentals and Advances.

This book offers a comprehensive overview of supervised and unsupervised algorithms, deep neural networks, and federated learning. In addition to addressing issues of ethics and explainability of models.

12.11   Inside Synthetic Minds.

This book reveals how these 'synthetic minds' are redefining creativity, work, and human interactions. This work presents a detailed analysis of the challenges and opportunities provided by these technologies, exploring their profound impact on society.

12.12   The Issue of Copyright.

This book invites the reader to explore the future of creativity in a world where human-machine collaboration is a reality, addressing questions about authorship, originality, and intellectual property in the age of generative AIs.

12.13   1121 Questions and Answers: From Basic to Complex – Part 1 to 4.

Organized into four volumes, these questions serve as essential practical guides to mastering key AI concepts.

Part 1 addresses information, data, geoprocessing, the evolution of artificial intelligence, its historical milestones and basic concepts.

Part 2 delves into complex concepts such as machine learning, natural language processing, computer vision, robotics, and decision algorithms.

Part 3 addresses issues such as data privacy, work automation, and the impact of large-scale language models (LLMs).

Part 4 explores the central role of data in the age of artificial intelligence, delving into the fundamentals of AI and its applications in areas such as mental health, government, and anti-corruption.

12.14 The Definitive Glossary of Artificial Intelligence.

This glossary presents more than a thousand artificial intelligence concepts clearly explained, covering topics such as Machine Learning, Natural Language Processing, Computer Vision, and AI Ethics.

- Part 1 conAnswerss concepts starting with the letters A to D.
- Part 2 conAnswerss concepts initiated by the letters E to M.
- Part 3 conAnswerss concepts starting with the letters N to Z.

12.15 Prompt Engineering - Volumes 1 to 6.

This collection covers all the fundamentals of prompt engineering, providing a complete foundation for professional development.

With a rich variety of prompts for areas such as leadership, digital marketing, and information technology, it offers practical examples to improve clarity, decision-making, and gain valuable insights.

The volumes cover the following subjects:

- Volume 1: Fundamentals. Structuring Concepts and History of Prompt Engineering.
- Volume 2: Security and Privacy in AI.
- Volume 3: Language Models, Tokenization, and Training Methods.
- Volume 4: How to Ask Right Questions.
- Volume 5: Case Studies and Errors.
- Volume 6: The Best Prompts.

12.16 Guide to Being a Prompt Engineer – Volumes 1 and 2.

The collection explores the advanced fundamentals and skills required to be a successful prompt engineer, highlighting the benefits, risks, and the critical role this role plays in the development of artificial intelligence.

Volume 1 covers crafting effective prompts, while Volume 2 is a guide to understanding and applying the fundamentals of Prompt Engineering.

12.17 Data Governance with AI – Volumes 1 to 3.

Find out how to implement effective data governance with this comprehensive collection. Offering practical guidance, this collection covers everything from data architecture and organization to protection and quality assurance, providing a complete view to transform data into strategic assets.

Volume 1 addresses practices and regulations. Volume 2 explores in depth the processes, techniques, and best practices for conducting effective audits on data models. Volume 3 is your definitive guide to deploying data governance with AI.

12.18 Algorithm Governance.

This book looks at the impact of algorithms on society, exploring their foundations and addressing ethical and regulatory issues. It addresses transparency, accountability, and bias, with practical solutions for auditing and monitoring algorithms in sectors such as finance, health, and education.

12.19 From IT Professional to AI Expert: The Ultimate Guide to a Successful Career Transition.

For Information Technology professionals, the transition to AI represents a unique opportunity to enhance skills and contribute to the development of innovative solutions that shape the future.

In this book, we investigate the reasons for making this transition, the essential skills, the best learning path, and the prospects for the future of the IT job market.

12.20 Intelligent Leadership with AI: Transform Your Team and Drive Results.

This book reveals how artificial intelligence can revolutionize team management and maximize organizational performance.

By combining traditional leadership techniques with AI-powered insights, such as predictive analytics-based leadership, you'll learn how to optimize processes, make more strategic decisions, and create more efficient and engaged teams.

12.21 Impacts and Transformations: Complete Collection.

This collection offers a comprehensive and multifaceted analysis of the transformations brought about by Artificial Intelligence in contemporary society.

- Volume 1: Challenges and Solutions in the Detection of Texts Generated by Artificial Intelligence.

- Volume 2: The Age of Filter Bubbles. Artificial Intelligence and the Illusion of Freedom.
- Volume 3: Content Creation with AI - How to Do It?
- Volume 4: The Singularity Is Closer Than You Think.
- Volume 5: Human Stupidity versus Artificial Intelligence.
- Volume 6: The Age of Stupidity! A Cult of Stupidity?
- Volume 7: Autonomy in Motion: The Intelligent Vehicle Revolution.
- Volume 8: Poiesis and Creativity with AI.
- Volume 9: Perfect Duo: AI + Automation.
- Volume 10: Who Holds the Power of Data?

12.22 Big Data with AI: Complete Collection.

The collection covers everything from the technological fundamentals and architecture of Big Data to the administration and glossary of essential technical terms.

The collection also discusses the future of humanity's relationship with the enormous volume of data generated in the databases of training in Big Data structuring.

- Volume 1: Fundamentals.
- Volume 2: Architecture.
- Volume 3: Implementation.
- Volume 4: Administration.
- Volume 5: Essential Themes and Definitions.
- Volume 6: Data Warehouse, Big Data, and AI.

13 About the Author.

I'm Marcus Pinto, better known as Prof. Marcão, a specialist in information technology, information architecture and artificial intelligence.

With more than four decades of dedicated work and research, I have built a solid and recognized trajectory, always focused on making technical knowledge accessible and applicable to all those who seek to understand and stand out in this transformative field.

My experience spans strategic consulting, education and authorship, as well as extensive performance as an information architecture analyst.

This experience enables me to offer innovative solutions adapted to the constantly evolving needs of the technological market, anticipating trends and creating bridges between technical knowledge and practical impact.

Over the years, I have developed comprehensive and in-depth expertise in data, artificial intelligence, and information governance –

areas that have become essential for building robust and secure systems capable of handling the vast volume of data that shapes today's world.

My book collection, available on Amazon, reflects this expertise, addressing topics such as Data Governance, Big Data, and Artificial Intelligence with a clear focus on practical applications and strategic vision.

Author of more than 150 books, I investigate the impact of artificial intelligence in multiple spheres, exploring everything from its technical bases to the ethical issues that become increasingly urgent with the adoption of this technology on a large scale.

In my lectures and mentorships, I share not only the value of AI, but also the challenges and responsibilities that come with its implementation – elements that I consider essential for ethical and conscious adoption.

I believe that technological evolution is an inevitable path. My books are a proposed guide on this path, offering deep and accessible insights for those who want not only to understand, but to master the technologies of the future.

With a focus on education and human development, I invite you to join me on this transformative journey, exploring the possibilities and challenges that this digital age has in store for us.

14 How to Contact Prof. Marcão.

14.1 For lectures, training and business mentoring.

marcao.tecno@gmail.com

14.2 Prof. Marcão, on Linkedin.

https://bit.ly/linkedin_profmarcao

www.ingramcontent.com/pod-product-compliance
Lightning Source LLC
LaVergne TN
LVHW022355060326
832902LV00022B/4450